Ancient E

PYRAMIDS

by Anne Giulieri

a Capstone company — publishers for children

Engage Literacy is published in the UK by Raintree.
Raintree is an imprint of Capstone Global Library Limited, a company incorporated in England and Wales
having its registered office at 264 Banbury Road, Oxford, OX2 7DY – Registered company number: 6695582

www.raintree.co.uk

Editorial credits
Gina Kammer, editor; Cynthia Della-Rovere (cover) and Peggie Carley (interior), designers;
Pam Mitsakos, media researcher; Tori Abraham, production specialist

Image credits
Alamy: Danita Delimont, 17, Images of Africa Photobank, 15; Bridgeman Images: De Agostini Picture Library/G. Dagli
Orti, 19 top right, Horse ring of Ramesses II (gold), Egyptian New Kingdom 19th Dynasty (c.1292-1187 BC)/Louvre,
Paris, France, 16; Capstone Press: Capstone Press, 7 top right; Getty Images: De Agostini Picture Library, 12 inset, De
Agostini/A. Dagli Orti, 8 bottom left, De Agostini/Chomon & Perino, 12-13 bottom, Design Pics/Deddeda, 9, Jochen
Schlenker/robertharding, 14; Shutterstock: ALEXANDER LEONOV, 4 top right, Andrea Izzotti, back cover, annarepp,
design element, attaphong, 4 top left, Fedor Selivanov, design element, FineShine, 1, Four Oaks, 10, Gilmanshin, 20-21,
holbox, 4 bottom right, Juriah Mosin, 18-19, Kues, design element, NaughtyNut, 5 bottom right, Nestor Noci, 8 bottom
right, WitR, cover top, 6-7; SuperStock: age fotostock, 22, ClassicStock.com, 11, DeAgostini, 23

10 9 8 7 6 5 4 3 2 1
Printed and bound in China.

Ancient Egyptian Pyramids

ISBN: 978 1 4747 3163 8

Contents

Pyramids

A pyramid is an odd shape. It has a square base and triangle-shaped sides. The sides join together at the top to make a point.

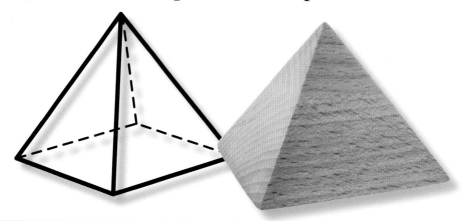

Did you know?

Some of the oldest pyramids were called step pyramids because they look like giant steps.

This pyramid is a
↓   step pyramid.

Around the world many different types of pyramids have been built. Pyramids can be found in the countries of Egypt, China, India and Mexico.

Some pyramids are very, very old, while other pyramids are not. Not all pyramids look exactly the same.

Did you know?

There are new pyramids, too.
A glass pyramid was built in France.

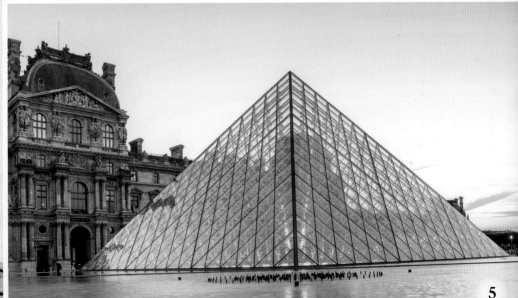

Ancient Egyptian Pyramids

The best-known pyramids are found in the country of Egypt. These pyramids were built on the bank of the River Nile. They were built thousands and thousands of years ago. We call the pyramids in Egypt *ancient* because they are very, very old.

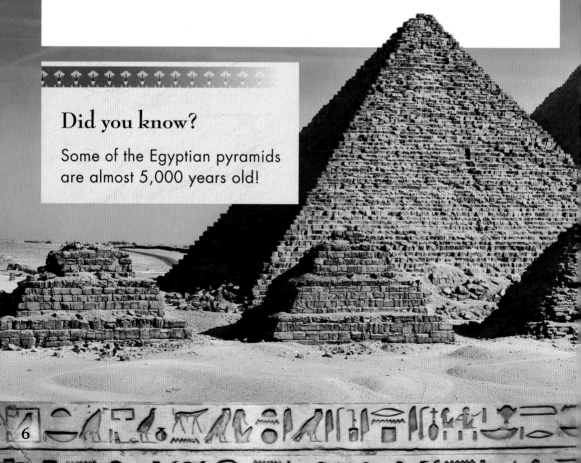

Did you know?

Some of the Egyptian pyramids are almost 5,000 years old!

Mediterranean Sea

Pyramids of Giza↗ ●Cairo

River Nile→

Red Sea

N

ANCIENT EGYPT

0   100   200 Miles
0   100   200   300 Kilometres

Did you know?

People who live in Egypt are called Egyptians.

The ancient Egyptians built pyramids to use as *tombs*. A tomb is a place where a body can be put after a person has died. The pyramids were built as tombs for the kings and queens of ancient Egypt. The ancient Egyptians called their kings and queens *pharaohs*. Although the pharaohs were buried in special tombs, most Egyptians were buried in the sand!

Did you know?

Some tombs were built into the sides of mountains.

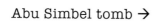
Abu Simbel tomb →

The ancient Egyptian pyramids were made of stone. The stone was cut into blocks. Each block needed to be exactly the right size and shape to fit the pyramids. Some of the smaller blocks were the size of a suitcase, while other blocks were as big as a car.

How were the pyramids built?

If the pyramids were built today, bulldozers, cranes and lorries would be used. These machines would help the builders to collect, move and place the blocks of stone.

Did you know?

The Great Pyramid is made from well over 2 million blocks.

But the pyramids were built thousands of years ago, and these machines didn't exist. So the people had to be very clever and find other ways to collect, move and place the large stones. They might have brought the stone on ships. They also might have used wooden sledges and ramps to move the stone.

WHAT'S INSIDE A PYRAMID?

Inside the pyramids are many tunnels and rooms. A tunnel inside a pyramid is called a passage, and a room is called a chamber.

Some of the passages are long and others are short. Some passages go up and some go down. You have to go through the passages to get to the chambers.

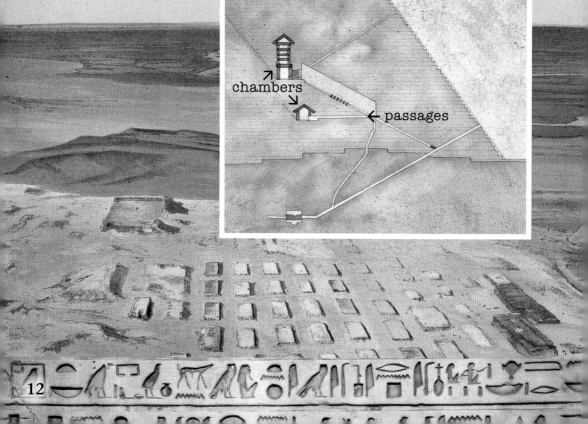

chambers

passages

When a pharaoh died, the ancient Egyptians would place his body in a special chamber inside the pyramid. Some of his belongings were also placed in this chamber. This was called a burial chamber. There were other chambers in the pyramids, too.

The pharaoh's family members were buried in nearby tombs. Sometimes they had smaller pyramids of their own.

The only way to get inside a pyramid was through a narrow passage. Often the entrance to the passage was hard to find. The entrance was hidden to keep the pharaoh and his belongings safe from *grave robbers*. Sometimes there were secret passages and stone doors inside the pyramids to try to stop robbers, too!

Did you know?

Even though there were secret passages, most of the pyramids were damaged, and grave robbers took many things.

The ancient Egyptians put lots of everyday items inside the pyramids. There they would place items that were important to the pharaoh. These included items such as vases, clothes, beds and food. Gold, silver and *jewels* would be placed in the tomb, too.

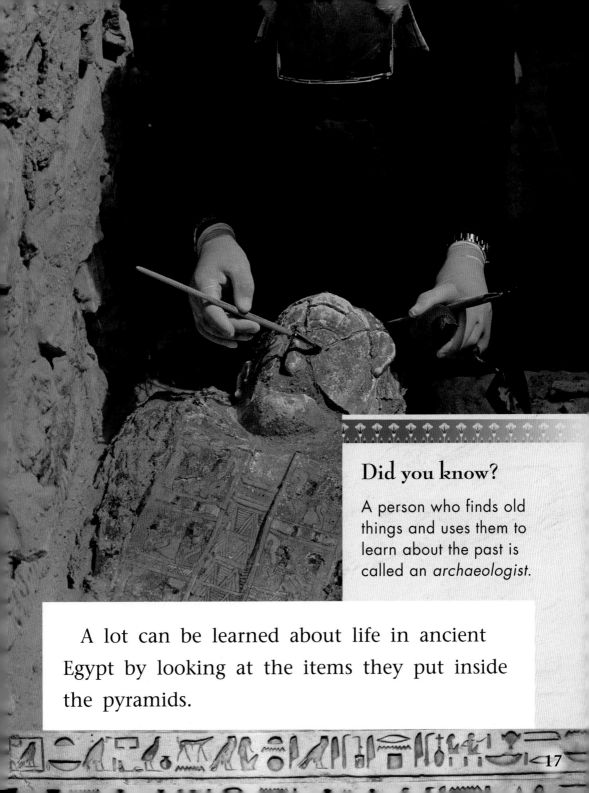

Did you know?

A person who finds old things and uses them to learn about the past is called an *archaeologist*.

A lot can be learned about life in ancient Egypt by looking at the items they put inside the pyramids.

Mummies

The ancient Egyptians did special things to take care of the bodies they put inside the pyramids. They rubbed lotion on them and then *wrapped* them in strips of cloth.

Did you know?

The pharaoh's body was mummified. This means that the body was *preserved*. "Preserved" means to make something last or keep.

They used a glue, made from plants, to keep the strands of cloth wrapped around the body. We call these ancient Egyptian bodies *mummies*.

Did you know?

Sometimes even animals such as cats, dogs and crocodiles were made into mummies. They were put inside the tombs, too.

Special Pictures

Inside the pyramids, there are lots of special pictures called *hieroglyphics*. These pictures are used to tell stories.

They tell stories about pharaohs and life in ancient Egypt. Some of these pictures were carved on stone, and others were painted on paper.

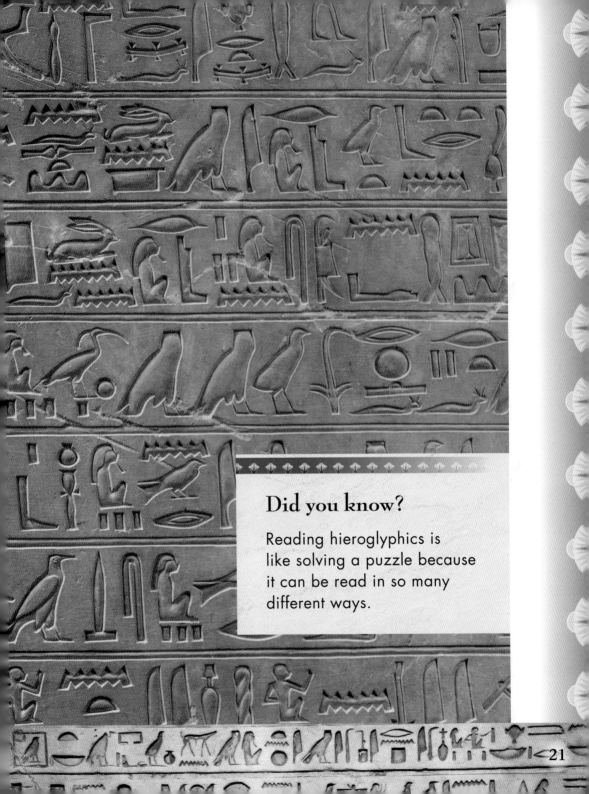

Big Time Capsules

By looking at the pyramids and all the things inside them, we have found out a lot about the ancient Egyptians. Many of the things that were inside the pyramids can now be seen in *museums*. Egyptian items in museums include animal statues, board games, jars, make-up boxes and jewellery.

Make-up boxes used by ancient Egyptians

Ancient Egyptians saved many of these treasures and belongings in pyramids. Some of these things stayed safe, so we can still see them today. A pyramid is like a giant *time capsule*. It can show us what life was like in Egypt thousands of years ago.

Glossary

ancient from a long time ago

archaeologist a person who learns about the past by digging up old buildings or objects and studying them

grave robber a person who steals valuable items from places where dead people are buried

hieroglyphics a form of writing in ancient Egypt that uses picture symbols

jewel a precious stone

mummy a body that has been preserved with special lotions and cloth

museum place where things from the past are displayed

pharaoh a king of ancient Egypt

preserve to make something last or keep

time capsule a box or other container that holds objects that tell things about people in a certain time; time capsules are left for people in the future to find

tombs a place where a person's body is put after the person has died

wrap to wind a covering, such as cloth, around something

Index